BUILDING YOUR HOUSE ON THE LORD

MARRIAGE & PARENTHOOD

13 Studies for Individuals or Groups

S T E V E & D E E B R E S T I N

Harold Shaw Publishers • Wheaton, Illinois

Copyright © 1976, 1980, revised edition 1993 by Harold Shaw Publishers

ISBN 0-87788-099-9

Cover photo © 1993 by Luci Shaw

99 98 97 96 95 94

15 14 13

CONTENTS

INTRODUCTION

Most Bible studyguides on marriage are written from one of two perspectives: the *hierarchical* or the *egalitarian*. When Dee surveyed 4,000 Christian women for her book *The Lifestyles of Christian Women*, she asked them:

> Which would you say most closely describes your marriage?
>
> a)____Egalitarian (We are coheirs and mutually submissive to each other)
>
> b)____Hierarchical (My husband is the head of the house, and I submit to him unless he delegates an area to me)

Intriguingly, 40 percent of the women checked egalitarian, 35 percent checked hierarchical, and 25 percent checked both!

Which view is more biblical? And are the two mutually exclusive? It is not unusual to find two seemingly conflicting views in Scripture. For example, it is clear we are saved by grace, and yet it is also clear that works are evidence of saving faith. Likewise, both free will and predestination are rich in scriptural support. Abuse occurs, we believe, when the proponents of one viewpoint seem unwilling to consider the scriptural support for the other viewpoint. The healthiest view seems to us to be a balance, and we are excited about providing a studyguide that considers both views on marriage. You will find those viewpoints discussed primarily in the Leader's Notes.

The prevailing theme of Scripture on marriage is not "Who's in charge here?" but "The two shall be one flesh." If we can give the concept of unity the priority it deserves and apply it in our attitudes and decisions, perhaps the other conflict (hierarchical vs. egalitarian) will fade away.

A house divided, Jesus warned, will not stand (Matthew 12:25)! He also warned of the folly of hearing God's Word but failing to apply it, likening that to a man who builds his house upon the sand. However, if we hear God's Word *and* apply it, Jesus said that though the rains fall and the floods rise, our house will not fall, for it is founded on the rock.

We have been married for over twenty-eight years and have a marriage rich in love, communication, and ministry. We are seeing our five children grow up to love and serve God, and have found the teachings of our Lord trustworthy and reliable. Come with us and learn how to build your house on the Lord.

HOW TO USE THIS STUDYGUIDE

Fisherman studyguides are based on the inductive approach to Bible study. Inductive study is discovery study; we discover what the Bible says as we ask questions about its content and search for answers. This is quite different from the process in which a teacher *tells* a group *about* the Bible and what it means and what to do about it. In inductive study God speaks directly to each of us through his Word.

A group functions best when a leader keeps the discussion on target, but this leader is neither the teacher nor the "answer person." A leader's responsibility is to *ask*—not *tell*. The answers come from the text itself as group members examine, discuss, and think together about the passage.

There are four kinds of questions in each study. The first is an *approach question*. Used before the Bible passage is read, this question breaks the ice and helps you focus on the topic of the Bible study. It begins to reveal where thoughts and feelings need to be transformed by Scripture.

Some of the earlier questions in each study are *observation questions* designed to help you find out basic facts—who, what, where, when, and how.

When you know what the Bible says you need to ask, *What does it mean?* These *interpretation questions* help you to discover the writer's basic message.

Application questions ask, *What does it mean to me?* They challenge you to live out the Scripture's life-transforming message.

Fisherman studyguides provide spaces between questions for jotting down responses and related questions you would like to raise in the group. Each group member should have a copy of the studyguide and may take a turn in leading the group.

A group should use any accurate, modern translation of the Bible such as the *New International Version*, the *New American Standard Bible*, the *Revised Standard Version*, the *New Jerusalem Bible*, or the *Good News Bible*. (Other translations or paraphrases of the Bible may be referred to when additional help is needed.) Bible commentaries should not be brought to a Bible study because they tend to dampen discussion and keep people from thinking for themselves.

SUGGESTIONS FOR GROUP LEADERS

1. Read and study the Bible passage thoroughly beforehand, grasping its themes and applying its teachings for yourself. Pray that the Holy Spirit will "guide you into truth" so that your leadership will guide others.

2. If the studyguide's questions ever seem ambiguous or unnatural to you, rephrase them, feeling free to add others that seem necessary to bring out the meaning of a verse.

3. Begin (and end) the study promptly. Start by asking someone to pray for God's help. Remember, the Holy Spirit is the teacher, not you!

4. Ask for volunteers to read the passages out loud.

5. As you ask the studyguide's questions in sequence, encourage everyone to participate in the discussion. If some are silent, ask, "What do you think, Heather?" or, "Dan, what can you add to that answer?" or suggest, "Let's have an answer from someone who hasn't spoken up yet."

6. If a question comes up that you can't answer, don't be afraid to admit that you're baffled! Assign the topic as a research project for someone to report on next week.

7. Keep the discussion moving and focused. Though tangents will inevitably be introduced, you can bring the discussion back to the topic at hand. Learn to pace the discussion so that you finish a study each session you meet.

8. Don't be afraid of silences: some questions take time to answer and some people need time to gather courage to speak. If silence persists, rephrase your question, but resist the temptation to answer it yourself.

9. If someone comes up with an answer that is clearly illogical or unbiblical, ask him or her for further clarification: "What verse suggests that to you?"

10. Discourage Bible-hopping and overuse of cross-references. Learn all you can from *this* passage, along with a few important references suggested in the studyguide.

11. Some questions are marked with a ♦. This indicates that further information is available in the Leader's Notes at the back of the guide.

12. For further information on getting a new Bible study group started and keeping it functioning effectively, read Gladys Hunt's *You Can Start a Bible Study Group* and *Pilgrims in Progress: Growing through Groups* by Jim and Carol Plueddemann.

SUGGESTIONS FOR GROUP MEMBERS

1. Learn and apply the following ground rules for effective Bible study. (If new members join the group later, review these guidelines with the whole group.)

2. Remember that your goal is to learn all that you can *from the Bible passage being studied.* Let it speak for itself without using Bible commentaries or other Bible passages. There is more than enough in each assigned passage to keep your group productively occupied for one session. Sticking to the passage saves the group from insecurity and confusion.

3. Avoid the temptation to bring up those fascinating tangents that don't really grow out of the passage you are discussing. If the topic is of common interest, you can bring it up later in informal conversation following the study. Meanwhile, help each other stick to the subject!

4. Encourage each other to participate. People remember best what they discover and verbalize for themselves. Some people are naturally shyer than others, or they may be afraid of making a mistake. If your discussion is free and friendly and you show real interest in what other group members think and feel, they will be more likely to speak up. Remember, the more people involved in a discussion, the richer it will be.

5. Guard yourself from answering too many questions or talking too much. Give others a chance to express themselves. If you are one who participates easily, discipline yourself by counting to ten before you open your mouth!

6. Make personal, honest applications and commit yourself to letting God's Word change you.

THE FOUNDATION

Matthew 7:24-27; Psalm 127

As a young couple househunting in Seattle, we found my dream house. Perched high on a cliff above the magnificent waters of the Puget Sound, the view from every window was spectacular! The house itself was charming, with slanted ceilings, wood floors, and a huge stone fireplace. And, amazingly, the price was low!

There was only one problem. The soil beneath the front of the house was beginning to crumble. My cautious husband refused to buy. Five years later I was thankful, for that beautiful house had slipped down into the Sound.

People attempt to enhance their marriages in all kinds of ways—enrichment seminars, family room additions, or vacations to Disneyland. But none of these things, even though they may be good, will make up for what we should have established from the beginning: a home built on Jesus himself.

1. When you feel cornered by family troubles, what do you fantasize will make everything better?

Read Matthew 7:24-27.

2. Describe the response of a person who builds "on sand."

Describe the response of a person who builds "on the rock."

Have you stopped toiling anxiously and begun resting in the Lord? If so, share briefly the effect this transition has had in one specific area of your life.

3. What are some specific ways a home built on Jesus and his Word would be different from a home built on the "sand" of this world's philosophies and practices?

4. Have you personally begun building your life on the rock by repenting of your sins and receiving Jesus? If this has happened to you, briefly tell the group how it happened.

Read Psalm 127:1-2.

5. How does the psalmist describe the work of those who build their house apart from the Lord? What does this mean?

What determines the success of "house building"?

◆ **6.** What point is the psalmist making in verse 2?

What application is there for marriage? For something you are worrying about right now?

7. If you have founded your life on Jesus and are obeying him, there is no reason for you to be anxious. According to verse 2, what does God give the one he loves?

Read Psalm 127:3-5.

♦ 8. These verses explain the blessings children bring to a home. Why is it best to have your home founded on the Lord before children arrive?

9. How should your recognition that children are God's gift influence your attitude toward them?

10. According to verse 5, what parent is particularly blessed? How is this emphasis different from the typical emphasis today?

Note: A quiver usually holds five arrows!

◆ **11.** What blessing did a large family bring in the days of the psalmist (verse 5)? What special blessings accompany large families today?

How is it possible to have a large family and yet not be anxious? How should a couple go about planning the size of their family?

13. What have you learned about building a sturdy home that can help your marriage and family?

GOD'S BLUEPRINT FOR MARRIAGE

Genesis 1:26–2:25

A study by D. Jernigan and Steven Nock of the University of Virginia found that while attending church had a positive impact on marital stability, it didn't necessarily affect marital satisfaction. What did influence marital satisfaction was internal faith. In other words, it is possible—even common—for couples to attend church without having a strong commitment to Christ. At home, they do not pray together, or read Scripture together, or seek God's direction for their daily lives. However, those couples who do demonstrate internal faith are impressively different! Their homes radiate peace, love, and joy.

The very fact that you are seeking to understand God's blueprint for marriage is evidence of the kind of internal faith that leads to marital satisfaction. God's blueprint for marriage is very different from what the world has in mind.

1. Briefly describe some of society's expectations for marriage.

Read Genesis 1:26-31, the first creation account of man and woman.

♦ **2.** What two forms of life were created in God's image?
What were their joint responsibilities to be?

Read Genesis 2:1-25, the second creation account of man and woman.

3. Throughout his creation, God had repeatedly observed that what he had brought into being "was good." Now, for the first time, in verse 18, God said that something was "not good." What was not good?

What does this tell you about our human make-up? How did God change the situation?

◆ **4.** The word translated "helper" in verse 18 is a combination of two Hebrew words. *Ezer* is translated "help" but shouldn't be taken to mean inferiority, for it is sometimes used in reference to God. *Neged* means "one corresponding to." In practical terms, what does this word *helper* mean to you in your marriage?

5. How is our correspondence, our man/woman interdependence, established and illustrated by God in verses 21-23?

◆ **6.** What is the result of the truth of verse 23 (note the "for this reason" that joins it to verse 24)?

7. What do you think God meant when he told marriage partners to leave their parents? Why is this essential for a healthy marriage?

8. How should the knowledge that every married couple must eventually "leave" their parents influence your attitude toward your children when they marry?

How can you apply this now, before their marriage? Be specific.

♦ **9.** The literal meaning of the Hebrew *to be united to* (or *cleave*, KJV) is "to stick to—to be glued together." If you pull apart two pieces of paper that are glued together, they will both be torn. In light of this, why is the marriage bond so important? Why is its dissolution so serious?

10. How should the decision to be united to your marriage partner protect your marriage?

11. How should the knowledge that you and your spouse are "one flesh" affect your attitude toward each other? Be specific.

12. Give specific suggestions as to how a married couple could demonstrate oneness and interdependence in the following areas:

Parenting

Lovemaking

Financial decisions

13. What are some of the advantages of having a life's companion? Have you experienced this?

THE MARRED BLUEPRINT

Genesis 3:1-19

Most couples struggle, at least during some periods of their lives, with the feeling that their marriage is never going to be what they dreamed it would be: a portrait of Christian unity. Why is this? Is it just that they cannot measure up to standard? Or is there something more fundamental involved—a flaw that stretches across humanity like a giant fault under the earth's crust?

God's blueprint *was* marred at the very beginning—by sin. One of the effects of the Fall was that husbands and wives would "desire to dominate" the other instead of putting the other's needs above their own. Each would want his or her own way.

Yet Christ can help reverse the effects of the Fall. We have seen it happen in our marriage—and so can you!

1. What do you see as the main point of conflict between the sexes?

Read Genesis 3:1-6.

◆ **2.** In verse 1, how did the serpent cause doubt in Eve's mind? How does Satan cause doubt in our minds today concerning the authority of God's Word?

3. To what weakness in Eve did Satan appeal in verse 5?

4. How can pride cause trouble in our fellowship with God? in our fellowship with our spouse? (List several ways.)

Read Genesis 3:7-15.

5. In response to God's question (verse 11), whom did Adam blame? When God questioned Eve, whom did she blame? Who is to blame for your sin?

♦ **6.** What curse did God pronounce upon the serpent in verse 14?

Read Genesis 3:16-19.

Concerning the consequences of the Fall, hierarchical and egalitarian proponents hold differing views. The following quotations represent the hierarchical and egalitarian perspectives respectively.

"The Bible teaches a subordination of the wife to her husband. In this, both Old and New Testaments agree. This subordination is grounded upon the creation. 'Adam was formed first, then Eve.' It is further grounded upon the fall of our first parents: 'Adam was not deceived (as long as he stood alone), but the woman was deceived and became a transgressor' (1 Timothy 2:13-14). After the Fall, upon each was laid a particular burden. The subordination of the wife was confirmed, indeed it was increased. (See Genesis 3:16-19.) We may strive against these words as much as we please. They are, and ever will be, the primitive law which has never ceased to be valid. Fallen man must submit to it, unless he would depart yet further from God." (Larry Christenson, *The Christian Family,* pp. 39-40. Minneapolis: Bethany Fellowship, 1970)

"In the past, we have taken this prediction of sin's result (Genesis 3:16-19) and have tried to institutionalize it and enforce it as God's will for us. Instead, we should be working to reverse it (as we have the other results of the Fall) and reinstate that lost relationship of mutual responsibility and respect that was present before the Fall.

God provided a Savior to mend the broken relationship between His human creation and Himself. Now He wants to work through us, His creation, to reverse the bad effects of the Fall. It is time we worked with Him to reinstate the original relationship between man and woman in marriage." (Patricia Gundry, *Heirs Together,* p. 88. Grand Rapids, Mich.: Zondervan, 1980)

♦ **7.** How do you see the Fall affecting your marriage or those of people you know?

♦ **8.** What consequences of the Fall are seen in the following verses?

> "I will greatly increase your pains in childbearing; with pain you will give birth to children.Your desire will be for your husband, and he will rule over you" (Genesis 3:16).

(The word translated "desire" can also be translated "desire to dominate.")

9. Can you think of ways in which the effects of the Fall can be reversed through Christ? Be specific.

10. In what ways do husbands and wives vie for authority in our society? What consequences does this sinful attitude have on a relationship?

11. Do you ever "desire to dominate," to have things your own way? Are you ever manipulative? Give some specific examples.

12. God's design, from the very beginning, was for husband and wife to work together as one. How is this partnership affected by submission, or lack of submission, to God?

13. Jesus said a "household divided against itself will not stand" and yet sin often divides our homes. Read Philippians 2:1-5 and then, in your own words, explain what steps a divided couple could take to restore Christian unity in their marriage.

A PATTERN FOR LIFE

Ephesians 5:1-17

Most of us have heard the "nature-nurture" arguments. Is our behavior mainly a result of inherited traits and tendencies? Or are we primarily the products of our environment? The Bible says, "Both."

We've inherited the human tendency for rebellion and destruction, which is why God made it possible to be "born again"—we actually *inherit* a new set of traits from our heavenly Father when the Holy Spirit comes to live in us.

At the same time, God is concerned about our environment and training. Much of the New Testament—including this study's passage—tells us how we can *nurture* our new *nature!*

1. Name a healthy pattern for expressing love that you learned from your parents. If you remember mostly negative patterns, give what you think would be their positive counterparts.

Read Ephesians 5:1-2.

2. List the commands given in verses 1-2.

3. What example are we given in verse 2? How is this different from the world's pattern for relating to people?

4. Give some specific examples of how you might "live a life of love"—following Christ's example in relating to your husband or wife.

Read Ephesians 5:3-10.

5. List, in your own words, all the kinds of behavior and conversation that would be unfitting in a Christian home (verses 3-5). What particularly stands out to you?

6. List the kinds of behavior that are fitting in a Christian home (verses 4, 8-10). What particularly stands out to you?

7. A Christian family can be a haven from the storms of the world. What are some specific ways you might strengthen your spouse or children for their encounters with outside pressures?

8. The Greek noun in verse 7 means "partaker." Check your dictionary. What does *partake* mean? In what should a believer not partake? Pornography and astrology are two examples of activities of darkness—what are some others? What reason is given for not partaking in these (verses 8-9)?

9. The RSV translates verse 10: "And try to learn what is pleasing to the Lord." How can you go about doing this?

Read Ephesians 5:11-17.

♦ **10.** J. B. Phillips paraphrases verse 11: "Steer clear of the fruitless activities of darkness; let your lives expose their futility." Can you think of a specific example of how a Christian family's way of life might show this contrast to the world?

11. Why should we walk wisely and carefully (verses 15-17)? Have you ever lost time because you acted impulsively without seeking the Lord's guidance? If so, explain.

12. God wants so much more than families who go through the rituals of churchgoing, praying before meals, and appearing to be nice. He wants *transformed* hearts, where members of a family are walking in sacrificial love toward one another and daily seeking his will. As you read verses 1-17 once again, what does God impress on your heart?

RESTORING THE ORIGINAL BLUEPRINT

Ephesians 4:1-6, 15-16; 5:18–6:4

Married couples who are Christians have a distinct advantage over those who are not Christians—if only they recognize it and learn to apply it to their lives. All married couples enjoy the unity that comes with physical intimacy, and many couples develop unity as friends and partners. But Christians can enjoy a unity of spirit—a union so mysterious that Bible writers use the marriage bond to try and describe it. The Christian is not only one body with spouse, but one body with all believers in Christ. The purpose of this study is to explore how spiritual realities can and should affect all other realities—including the marriage union.

1. What insight have you been able to bring to your marriage from your faith in Christ?

Read Ephesians 4:1-6, 15-16.

   2. Based upon these passages, describe how our behavior toward one another should be influenced by the knowledge that we are "one body." Be specific.

♦ **3.** In verses 15-16, Christ is described as being the Head from whom the whole body grows and is joined together. How is this concept related to our oneness as a body of believers?

Read Ephesians 5:18-21.

♦ **4.** What should stimulate and control a believer? What should not? Based upon Scripture, what would you say is the key to a Spirit-controlled life?

5. The following verses describe Spirit-filled behavior. What do they say a Spirit-filled person is like?

verse 19

verse 20

verse 21

6. How is being Spirit-controlled related to submission?

7. Verse 21 is foundational for the rest of the passage. The King James Version gives a very literal translation from the Greek: "Submitting yourselves one to another in the fear of God." What does this mean?

8. If possible, share an example from your life when you were tempted to go "your own way" but instead, through obedience to the Spirit, put your spouse's needs ahead of your own.

9. Read the following verses and discuss how they relate to mutual submission between husband and wife:

"But since there is so much immorality, each man should have his own wife, and each woman her own husband. The husband should fulfill his marital duty to his wife, and likewise the wife to her husband. The wife's body does not belong to her alone but also to her husband. In the same way, the husband's body does not belong to him alone but also to his wife." (1 Corinthians 7:2-4)

"In the Lord, however, woman is not independent of man, nor is man independent of woman. For as woman came from man, so also man is born of woman. But everything comes from God." (1 Corinthians 11:11-12)

Read Ephesians 5:22-33.

10. According to verses 28-30, how should the knowledge that you are "one body" with your spouse affect your behavior toward him (or her)? Be specific.

♦ 11. What can we learn from this comparison between Christ and his bride, the church, and husband and wife concerning:

the attitude a wife should have toward her husband?

the attitude a husband should have toward his wife?

the oneness of husband and wife?

the leadership of the husband?

12. Verse 33 reads, literally, "However, each one of you also must love his wife as he loves himself, in order that the wife respect her husband." Using specific illustrations, describe the kind of loving behavior that draws respect from a wife.

13. Do you see both the egalitarian and hierarchical perspectives in Ephesians 5? If so, how? Do you think they are incompatible?

Read Ephesians 6:1-4.

14. What commandment is given to children? To fathers? What does this mean? How might this apply to you specifically?

15. What impact do you think the relationship of husband and wife has on the children in a family?

MARRIAGE IN DIFFICULT CIRCUMSTANCES

1 Peter 2:21–3:1-7, 13-17; 4:7-17

While many marriages are, as the saying goes, "made in heaven," all of them must exist in a fallen world. Every aspect of our lives is subject to changes over which we have little or no control—the economy, our health, the political climate, our emotional and mental well-being, even difficulties in the local or regional church. Some of the most frightening changes occur within the marriage itself, as one or the other partner experiences shifts in health, career, or spiritual growth.

The early Christians didn't have sophisticated language (mid-life crises, corporate buy-outs) by which to label the trials they experienced, but they had to learn the same principles we do today as we deal with life's ups and downs—and all within the context of married life.

1. Name a struggle connected to married life that you were unprepared for.

Read 1 Peter 2:21-25.

2. When Christ suffered, he left an example for believers to follow. How did he react? In whom did he trust?

In what specific ways, then, should we "follow in his steps?"

3. Jesus' suffering was an example for us—but it was much more. What was the threefold purpose of his crucifixion (verse 24)? What does this mean to you personally, and to your marriage?

Read 1 Peter 3:1-7.

♦ 4. To whom are wives to submit? What reason for optimism is given to wives of unbelieving husbands?

How do you think a woman with an unbelieving husband can avoid being weakened by him and instead grow stronger spiritually?

5. Why did Peter emphasize winning a spouse by behavior, not by talk, in this situation?

♦ **6.** Why do you think verses 3-6 come directly after 1-2? How might the wife of an unbelieving husband be tempted to act in order to influence him?

How do you think a woman making a claim to godliness should dress and "adorn" herself today?

◆ **7.** In verse 7, Peter is speaking to believing husbands. He begins with the word *Likewise,* referring again to the examples of submission given already in this letter. In what way(s) do you think women are weaker, as mentioned here?

8. If a man abuses his position as head of the home and does not treat his wife considerately, what will happen to his communication with God?

Read 1 Peter 3:13-17.

◆ **9.** Who is likely to harm you if you are pleasing the Lord (verse 13)? But if you are criticized how should you feel about it?

◆ **10.** In what way are we to be prepared, according to verse 15? What is our attitude to be?

Read 1 Peter 4:7-17.

11. In light of the world situation, what are we instructed to do in verses 7-10?

12. According to verses 12-17, what can we expect as Christians who live in the world?

13. What encouragement are we given?

UNDERSTANDING GOD'S VIEW OF DIVORCE

Matthew 19:3-12; Malachi 2:11-16; 1 Corinthians 7:10-16

Research shows that after an initial period of relief, most divorced couples regret their decision. And although there are scriptural reasons for divorce, it still breaks God's heart. We have better understood God's hatred of divorce because of the honest testimonies of two of our friends:

Mike: I lost my daughters. Oh, I had them every other weekend—but they resented the disruption in their lives. And they blamed me. They still do, though it's been fourteen years. I reflect back to the things I did wrong, and how I contributed to the divorce, and I'm filled with guilt. It all happened so suddenly, yet the consequences go on and on. Money, weddings, Christmas . . . endless tension and pain.

Beth: We fought about who'd get the picture albums—yet who really wants them? It's so painful to look at our once whole family. And the worst is that we've permanently damaged our children. Their chances of a happy marriage have been drastically reduced—the statistics verify that.

They dread the holidays, and I do too. I can't turn to my new husband and say, "Do you remember the Christmas when Johnny . . ." because David wasn't there. I am convinced God never intended us to leave our first love.

1. Look up the word *faithful* in a regular and/or Bible dictionary. Briefly discuss how the different definitions might apply to the marriage union.

Read Matthew 19:3-12.

2. What was the first question the Pharisees asked Jesus (verse 3)? Read Jesus' answer carefully and paraphrase it in your own words.

3. What was the Pharisees' second question (verse 7)?

♦ **4.** Why did Jesus say Moses permitted divorce? What does it mean to be hardhearted?

♦ **5.** From this passage, how do you think God views divorce?

6. What was the disciples' reaction to this statement concerning the permanency of marriage (verse 10)? How did Jesus answer them?

Read Malachi 2:11-16.

♦ **7.** Briefly summarize the situation described here. Why is God angry with the men of Israel?

8. How seriously had the Israelites taken their marriage vows (verse 14)? If you have made marriage vows before God, how seriously do you take them?

9. How do you react to God's strong statement about divorce in verse 16?

Read 1 Corinthians 7:10-16.

◆ **10.** Why should the believing partner stay with the unbelieving partner?

◆ **11.** According to verse 15, what should the believer do if the unbeliever wants to depart? Why?

Does the believing partner have any guarantee that his or her spouse will be saved (verse 16)?

12. Has this study of God's view of divorce affected your attitude toward your marriage? What steps would you take if you felt your marriage was in trouble?

God hates divorce, but he still loves those who have been divorced. Sometimes believers seem unforgiving toward those who have divorced, but God always offers forgiveness. Jesus tells us all sins (including divorce!) may be forgiven except blasphemy against the Holy Spirit (continual and total rejection of the Lord—Matthew 12:31). Donald Cole, a radio pastor, says, "Once the papers are signed, it's too late for rebukes, too late for the good advice which, at an earlier stage, might have saved the marriage. Compassion and acceptance are needed now" (Donald Cole, "What to Say to a Divorced Friend." Reprinted from the March issue of *Moody Monthly*, Moody Bible Institute of Chicago, 1976).

13. Meditate on the following passage from Philippians:

> "This one thing I do, forgetting those things which are behind, and reaching forth unto those things which are before, I press toward the mark for the prize of the high calling of God in Christ Jesus." (Philippians 3:13-14, KJV)

How might this passage help the divorced person?

14. Proverbs 17:17 says that "a friend loveth at all times, and a brother is born for adversity." If you have been divorced, share how friends have been or could be more sensitive. If you have divorced friends, how can you show your love and compassion for them?

THE ROOT AND FRUIT OF LOVE IN THE FAMILY

John 15:1-17; 1 Corinthians 13:1-7

The average family has many demands on its time and energy. Those demands increase whenever the family tries to adhere to a faith system that brings with it high ideals. So it is no wonder that so many Christian families are exhausted and frustrated. But should it be so? Does being a "Christian family" simply mean that we try harder to be "good" people? How can we possibly fulfill the blueprint God has for us? What kind of resources do we have?

1. Briefly describe one of the most frustrating aspects of trying to be a Christian family.

Read John 15:1-8.

2. In looking at all these verses, what do you think Jesus is trying to get across?

3. What is the key to "bearing fruit"?

4. It is in our homes that the real "fruit" of our lives becomes evident, for there our true character, priorities, and activities become clear. With that in mind, what kind of fruit are you producing?

5. According to verse 8, what are two of the results of our bearing much fruit?

Read John 15:9-17.

6. According to verses 10-11, what is characteristic of the life of an obedient child of God?

7. Jesus has already explained that we must remain in him. Now he more specifically describes what he means. What are we to remain in? And how do we remain in it (verse 10)?

8. How are we described by Jesus in verses 13-15? How should this affect our approach to being fruitful people?

Read 1 Corinthians 13:1-7.

9. God gives spiritual gifts to his children. Of what profit are they if they are not exercised in love (verses 1-3)? When one serves his or her family without love, how worthwhile is that service to God?

10. Look at each characteristic described in verses 4-7 and think of home life situations to which it applies. What sins and failings need to be confessed in your family?

11. Look especially at verse 7. How does this description compare to the prevailing culture around you? What attitudes must you battle in order to fulfill God's kind of love?

◆ **12.** This passage describes love in its ideal, purest form. In light of this standard, how can Jesus' teaching about the vine and the branches be especially encouraging?

SPIRITUAL EXPRESSION IN THE FAMILY

Colossians 3:1-4; Ecclesiastes 4:9-12; Deuteronomy 6:4-9

Ask nearly any Christian leader about influences in his or her spiritual development, and the answer will be something simple: a mother who prayed over him every nigh; a grandfather who could be found any morning in his special chair, reading Scripture; a father who asked forgiveness whenever he wronged anyone—especially his wife and children; or a family practice of setting aside money for missions, or spending vacation time serving the poor or sick. These are the expressions of God's love that shape our lives.

1. Describe to the group one aspect—it can be positive or negative—of your spiritual heritage.

Read Colossians 3:1-4.

2. According to this passage, why should a believer in Christ be setting and seeking spiritual goals rather than earthly ones? Name some spiritual goals.

3. Describe some examples in which day-to-day living is transformed by a mindset "on things above." How can our focus be on heavenly goals without neglecting earthly duties?

4. What do these verses say about our future?

5. What kind of values exist in a home where goals are heavenly?

What habits in our home can demonstrate to our children what it means to set our minds on things above?

Read Ecclesiastes 4:9-12.

6. What are some of the advantages of having a partner?

How should a partnership mentality affect a family during difficult times? When someone is ill or under great stress?

7. If "two are better than one," three are better than two! In a Christian's marriage, that third partner can be God. If you pray with your spouse or study Scripture with your spouse, describe how you do it.

Read Deuteronomy 6:4-9.

♦ **8.** What did the Lord teach his people in verse 5?

In what ways might your life give evidence of this kind of love for the Lord?

9. Meditate on verse 7. What are the four opportunities mentioned for sharing spiritual truth with your children?

What does it mean to "impress them on your children"?

10. The Lord instructed his people to talk about his commandments "when you walk along the road." What might this mean for today's Christian family?

11. In addition to informal spiritual conversations throughout the day, a scheduled time of family devotions can be of real value. Describe some ways that family devotions could be conducted so that they would be both rewarding and enjoyable for the following age levels:

preschool

elementary

teenage

12. In verses 8-9 the Lord is telling believers to put reminders of him and his Word everywhere! How can we remind ourselves of God today?

What sets the climate of your home? Describe ways in which you can make your home a place of comfort, truth, and testimony to God.

PHYSICAL EXPRESSION IN MARRIAGE

Proverbs 5:15-21; 1 Corinthians 6:9–7:9

Oneness in marriage is beautifully illustrated by the way God created husband and wife to become one physically. Sex within the marital relationship is designed to be wonderful! A healthy sexual relationship bonds a couple, helps keep them from temptation, and helps them to practice putting the other's needs above their own. No wonder God tells us not to refuse each other!

Yet many couples neglect to put God's warnings into practice. Then when the rains come, and the floods rise, their houses fall, for they were built on the sand.

1. What kind of attitudes toward sex prevailed in your home when you were growing up?

Read Proverbs 5:15-21.

2. What is being encouraged in this passage?

What is being warned against?

♦ **3.** What do these verses imply about modesty? About privacy? Besides extramarital affairs, how are modesty and privacy sometimes violated in a marriage?

4. Is there anything in these verses that indicates sexual satisfaction is a wild, arbitrary thing over which we have no control? Can you think of ways in which a person can *choose* to be captivated by his or her partner's love?

5. From these verses, what seems to be God's view of sexual enjoyment?

Read 1 Corinthians 6:9-20.

6. Sexual sin seems to cause more guilt than other types of sin. A person who has repented (confessed and forsaken) his or her sin to God can enter into a blessed marital relationship. How does Paul describe this to us in verse 11?

7. Why is a Christian's involvement with a prostitute an abomination to the Lord (verses 15-17)?

8. How should the knowledge that you are part of Christ affect what you do with your body and mind?

9. What practical steps can you take to apply verse 18 to your life?

Read 1 Corinthians 7:1-9.

10. What is God's provision for both personal fulfillment and the problem of temptation?

11. Meditate on verses 3-4. Express what Paul is saying in your own words.

Why is a husband or wife who rejects the marriage partner sexually acting contrary to God's will? What is the root problem behind such rejection?

12. Couples may mutually decide to abstain from sex for a period of time (verse 5). For what purpose? For how long? Have you found this to be of value?

♦ **13.** What other methods, besides saying no, do we sometimes use to avoid sexual intimacy with our spouse? What does this kind of subtle rejection eventually do to a marriage? What kinds of communication patterns can we cultivate that would make it easier to face sexual fears and frustrations?

14. What principles studied in previous lessons can you apply specifically to the sexual relationship? Explain.

COMMUNICATION IN THE FAMILY

Ephesians 4:25-32; selected proverbs

They're walking down the aisle together, still in their workday clothes, and they both look irritated. It's aisle 11 in the grocery store—canned vegetables and sauces. There's some dispute over an item they missed. He was supposed to pick it up three aisles ago, but she never specified the brand name. Hateful words fly. She never gives the right information; he's forgetful and inconsiderate. She needs to plan better; and if he spent a little more time at home, he'd *know* what groceries they bought. The tone of their voices, drifting by the canned goods, is even uglier than the words themselves. If you look closely, you'll see their wedding bands. But you don't need to; only married people would talk to one another this way.

1. Name a verbal habit in your marriage you would like to change.

Read Ephesians 4:25-32.

2. What compelling reason for honesty is given in verse 25? Who are our closest "neighbors"?

What effect does dishonesty have on a husband-wife relationship? On a parent-child relationship?

♦ 3. Ephesians 4:15 says that we must "[speak] the truth in love." In what ways does truthfulness temper our emotions?

♦ 4. According to verses 26-27, how long does the Lord give you to get rid of your anger? Why? What happens if resentment is not dealt with right away?

5. Describe the kind of communication that is pleasing to God. In contrast, describe the kind of communication that grieves the Holy Spirit (verses 29-32).

6. In light of these verses, what kinds of verbal communication should parents watch out for in their children?

Because the use of the tongue (communication) is a prominent theme in the book of Proverbs, we've selected several verses that are pertinent to communication in the family. James 3:1-12 also gives helpful wisdom on the use of the tongue.

> "An anxious heart weighs a man down, but a kind word cheers him up." (Proverbs 12:25)

> "Pleasant words are a honeycomb, sweet to the soul and healing to the bones." (Proverbs 16:24)

7. What do you learn about encouragement from the above proverbs?

"Good people think before they answer. Evil people have a quick reply, but it causes trouble." (Proverbs 15:28, TEV)

"He who answers before listening—that is his folly and his shame" (Proverbs 18:13)

8. What do you learn about listening from the above proverbs? Describe a good listener.

How could you improve the way you listen to your spouse or children?

"A good man's words are like pure silver; a wicked man's ideas are worthless." (Proverbs 10:20, TEV)

9. Jesus tells us that our words reveal what is in our hearts (Matthew 12:33-35). List the most frequent topics of conversation in your home. Do these have a worthwhile effect on your family members?

What are some conversational topics that would be worthwhile? What can you do to help your family conversation into constructive patterns?

"A gentle answer turns away wrath, but a harsh word stirs up anger." (Proverbs 15:1)

"He who is slow to anger is better than the mighty, and he who rules his spirit than he who takes a city." (Proverbs 16:32, RSV)

"The start of an argument is like the first break in a dam; stop it before it goes any further." (Proverbs 17:14, TEV)

10. Summarize what these proverbs teach about arguments. If you have a quick temper, what are some specific things you can do to control it?

If someone in your family has a quick temper, how can you help him or her to cool down?

"A wise son heeds his father's instruction, but a mocker does not listen to rebuke." (Proverbs 13:1)

"Listen to advice and accept instruction, and in the end you will be wise." (Proverbs 19:20)

11. Why, according to these proverbs, should we listen to advice? Why is criticism so difficult for us to accept?

"Some people like to make cutting remarks, but the words of the wise soothe and heal." (Proverbs 12:18, TLB)

"She speaks with wisdom, and faithful instruction is on her tongue." (Proverbs 31:26)

12. What is the best approach in giving advice? What should be the motive behind the giving of advice?

13. Think about the reactions you receive when trying to instruct your children or talking with your spouse about household matters. What do their expressions indicate about the way you communicate? What improvements might you make?

THE CHRISTIAN FAMILY AND MONEY

Luke 12:13-34; 2 Corinthians 9:6-15; Malachi 3:2-12; Romans 13:6-8

Before we gave our lives to Christ, Steve and I spent our free time roaming the furniture store and sketching floor plans for the "dream house." When my sister Sally presented the gospel to me and said that Jesus wanted my whole life, I asked her if that would mean giving up our dream house. Pensively Sally said, "I think that, in your case, the house would have to go—because it seems to be an idol in your life."

When I surrendered my life (and my dream house!) to Christ, I was filled with a desire to lay up treasures in heaven instead of treasures on earth. When Steve came to Christ, his goals changed as well. We began to practice the scriptural principles of tithing, being free of debt, and seeing God provide for our needs.

Yet we still have so much materially. We have just adopted a twelve-year-old girl from Thailand. All of her possessions came in a 2′ x 3′ box. We have seen the starving children in Third World countries. When are we being selfish? How much is too much? And when are we being legalistic and miserly? What does the Bible really have to say about money?

1. If your financial situation were ideal in God's eyes, how do you think it would be different than it is now?

Read Luke 12:13-15.

2. What warning did Jesus give the two brothers who were arguing over their inheritance?

Jesus referred to "all kinds of greed." Name a few.

3. What are some specific ways you can help your children to appreciate a simple, unmaterialistic way of life? What can you do to curb your own tendency to materialism?

Read Luke 12:16-21.

4. What was the rich fool living for? Why was this short-sighted?

5. What kind of wealth should we set our sights on? How should this influence our career choices and our conversation with our children about their career choices?

6. Many passages in Scripture warn of the foolishness of making material possessions the goal of life. Paul tells us that "those who desire to be rich fall into temptation, into a snare, into many senseless and hurtful desires that plunge men into ruin and destruction" *(1 Timothy 6:9, RSV)*. Consider the snares of debt, dishonesty, or the stress of maintaining an affluent lifestyle. What "snares" have been in your life because of an unbalanced view of material goods?

Read Luke 12:22-34.

7. What is Jesus warning us against? How is he encouraging us?

8. God expects us to be responsible enough to provide for our families. He says, "If any provide not for his own, and specially for those of his own house, he hath denied the faith, and is worse than an infidel" (*1 Timothy 5:8, KJV*). If this responsibility weighs heavily on your shoulders, how might verses 28-31 be of comfort?

9. Verse 31 is a well-known verse. What does this mean? Have you applied this promise to your life and experienced its truth? Explain.

Read 2 Corinthians 9:6-15.

♦ **10.** Find everything you can in verses 6-11 about how and why you should give of your resources.

Find everything you can in verses 12-15 about the effects of giving.

Read Malachi 3:2-12.

11. How does God want us to bring our offerings to him (verse 3)?

Describe those who are often oppressed financially (verse 5), and talk about how God feels about this.

◆ **12.** What did God ask of the Israelites, and how does this apply to you (verses 6-12)?

Read Romans 13:6-8.

13. What principles about money do you find in this passage? How should you apply this to your life?

14. As a result of this study, do you see any changes that need to be made in your family financial patterns? What are they?

DISCIPLINING OUR CHILDREN

Hebrews 12:5-15; selected proverbs

Steve and I had one child when we came to Christ (now we have five). I had been reluctant to discipline our firstborn, as I falsely associated discipline with a lack of love. Because I was so permissive, J. R. was unruly, and Steve sometimes lost his temper with him. We were not united in our approach to discipline.

When J. R. began going to a Christian school in Ohio, a loving teacher took me aside and told me that if J. R. was to remain at that school, it was important for him to learn to respect authority. She showed me, scripturally, that setting boundaries and consistently enforcing them was an act of love—and that the undisciplined child grew up to have a life of woe.

Steve and I prayed about what boundaries were important, and together, in oneness, began to lovingly but firmly enforce them. That godly woman's counsel has helped produce a "harvest of righteousness" in our children's lives.

1. Recall a time when you received discipline that helped you to change bad behavior *or* was especially negative for you. What made it helpful or harmful?

Read Hebrews 12:5-8.

2. What does the discipline of the Lord prove to us?

Why is it a greater act of love to discipline children than to always let them follow their own inclinations?

> "If you refuse to discipline your son, it proves you don't love him; for if you love him you will be prompt to punish him." (Proverbs 13:24, TLB)

3. When parents are permissive, what lack in them does their unrestrained child sense? When a child tests boundaries we have set, what else is he or she testing?

Read Hebrews 12:9-11.

4. Meditate on verse 9. When children learn to respect and obey their earthly fathers, whom else are they learning to obey?

What other authority figures is each person likely to meet in life? How will respect for parents affect our relationships with authorities?

5. According to this Hebrews passage, what is the end purpose of God's discipline? What should always be your motive in disciplining your children?

◆ **6.** What are some of the differences between the way earthly parents discipline and the way God disciplines?

What should and shouldn't be present when we discipline our children?

7. What are some reasons parents avoid discipline (verse 11)?

> "Discipline your son, for in that there is hope;
> do not be a willing party to his death."
> (Proverbs 19:18)

How does a parent become "a willing party to his death" in not disciplining a child? Think of examples.

8. Reflect on verse 11 and explain what should be the motivation for disciplining and training our children. Then, together with your spouse, talk about what kind of fruit you would like to see developed in your children and what rules or practices you are willing to consistently enforce to see it happen. Describe your plans.

Read Hebrews 12:12-15.

♦ **9.** Each of us has "feeble arms" and "weak knees," areas of our lives that are not necessarily rooted in rebellion, but are weaknesses of character and practice. Name some areas of weakness that need to be attended to in your family.

♦ **10.** What is meant by verse 13? Give an example of a child being "disabled" for lack of discipline and training.

11. Some behavior in our children may not be displeasing to God but is irritating to us. Can you think of examples?

How should parents deal with this kind of behavior?

"Train a child in the way he should go, and
when he is old he will not turn from it."
(Proverbs 22:6)

12. Verse 14 tells us to strive for peace and holiness. Why
is it especially important for the parent who is disciplining his or her children to be simultaneously leading a
clean life, set apart for God?

◆ **13.** Verse 15 warns against allowing any "bitter root" to
spring up. Colossians 3:21 says "Fathers, do not embitter
your children, or they will become discouraged." What
kind of discipline leads to bitterness between child and
parent? (If you are not sure, ask your children what they
think is fair and unfair discipline.)

14. As your children approach adolescence, your discipline should allow for their changing needs and feelings. Describe some of the special needs and feelings you
had as an adolescent.

15. Describe one way you are better equipped to build your house on the Lord as a result of this study.

LEADER'S NOTES

■ **Study 1/The Foundation**

Question 6. A parallel passage is Matthew 6:25-34.

Question 8. Many parents commit their lives to the Lord long after their children have arrived. They should go to their children and confess that they have built their home on the wrong foundation. They need to ask their forgiveness and tell them they are now going to build on Christ and his Word. Such repentance (confessing and forsaking sin) is a tremendous witness.

Question 11. This is a gray area in Scripture, but if time permits, the following questions could provoke an edifying discussion: Did you and your husband pray and seek the Lord's will before you decided whether or not to conceive or adopt a child? Are there forms of birth control that you think are not pleasing to the Lord? If so, why?

■ **Study 2/God's Blueprint for Marriage**

Question 2. Those who hold to the egalitarian concept in marriage would emphasize the importance of God's original plan. Both man and woman were created in God's image, and together they were given dominion over the earth.

Question 4. Those who hold to the hierarchical concept of marriage would emphasize the word *ezer* (help) in this word. While this should not be overlooked, in this context, *neged* (one corresponding to) also needs emphasis. In the New Testament, when wives are told to submit to their husbands, the thought is similar to this word *neged*. Just as Eve was created "to correspond to" her husband, so wives are supposed to submit, "to fit in, to adapt to their husbands."

Question 6. Oneness seems to be the emphasis that permeates Scripture. Genesis 2:24 appears four times in the New Testament (Matthew 19:5; Mark 10:7-8; 1 Corinthians 6:16; Ephesians 5:31). Notice the three subconcepts in this verse: Leaving, cleaving, and becoming one flesh.

Question 9. "Cleaving means love . . . of a special kind. It is love which has made a decision and which is no longer a groping and seeking love. Love which cleaves is mature love, love which has decided to remain faithful—faithful to one person—and to share with this one person one's whole life" (Walter Trobisch, *I Married You,* p. 16. San Francisco: Harper & Row, 1971. Used by permission of the author).

■ Study 3/The Marred Blueprint

If it becomes apparent that those in the group hold strongly differing views, you might preface this study by saying: This is a topic upon which Christians who truly love the Lord disagree. Stopping the discussion would be frustrating, and continuing it might lead to an unedifying argument. We suggest that those who wish to, take turns expressing their views with brevity, love, and Scriptural support. Then when everyone has had a chance to summarize his or her position, we'll close the subject and go on to the next question."

Question 2. Those who hold to the hierarchical perspective of marriage would emphasize 1 Timothy 2:13-14 at this point. Because this is a difficult passage, we would suggest doing some outside reading on both perspectives.

Question 6. Genesis 3:15 is a well-known Scripture passage. In the middle of this account of the Fall and its consequences, God gives the first prophecy of his solution: There will be a lengthy struggle between humans and Satan, but eventually the seed of a woman (Mary's son Jesus) will crush Satan's head.

Question 7. In this point, it's impossible for us (Steve and Dee) to avoid taking a stand on interpretation. Here we agree with the egalitarian perspective. It does seem true to us that Christ is God's solution to our Fall and that we should allow his Spirit to reverse the effects of the Fall.

Question 8. Genesis 3:16 is difficult but important. The problem arises from the Hebrew word *shuqah,* which is here translated, simply, "desire." Elsewhere (the Song of Solomon) *shuqah* is translated "sexual desire." Some commentators prefer this interpretation here. If they are correct, sexual desire in marriage would have to be seen as a negative aftereffect of the Fall. *Shuqah* may also be translated "the desire to dominate, to herd," as in Genesis 4:7. This makes better sense here and fits with the context. Because of sin, woman would now desire to dominate her husband. And, correspondingly, because of sin, man would also desire to "rule over" his wife. God's plan of oneness has been marred.

■ **Study 4/A Pattern for Life**

Question 10: It is important to avoid evil pleasures, but we must go even further. Paul instructs us to rebuke and expose them, for often our silence is interpreted as approval. God needs people who will take a stand for what is right. Wherever you are, lovingly speak out for what is true and right.

■ Study 5/Restoring the Original Blueprint

Question 3. This word *head* (in Greek, *kephale*) is the same word that is used in reference to the husband in Ephesians 5:23. It is an important word, deserving thorough study.

Proponents of egalitarian marriage would emphasize that the word *head* in many passages (Ephesians 4:15-16; Colossians 1:17-18; 2:18-19) seems to be seen simply as the source of nourishment and harmony to the body of believers. This is certainly part of the definition.

But we cannot ignore the fact that the word *kephale* has connotations of authority and leadership elsewhere in Scripture. (See Matthew 21:42 and Ephesians 1:21-22, where it is often translated "cornerstone.") This perspective, which sees leadership in the word *head*, is strengthened by the analogy in Ephesians 5:23-32.

Question 4. One passage dealing with this is Romans 8:1-13.

Question 11. The leadership of the husband is further clarified in some verses outside this study's main passage: 1 Corinthians 11:3, 8-9; 1 Timothy 2:13-14; Titus 2:4-5.

There are those who would say the first two of these references are related to order in the church and not to marriage. In any case, these passages deserve further study.

■ Study 6/Marriage in Difficult Circumstances

Question 4. First Peter 3:1 begins with "In the same way." This phrase refers us back to chapter 2, where people are instructed to submit to the ruling authority and servants to their masters as Jesus submitted to his Father.

Question 6. A woman married to a non-Christian may think that holy living will have little effect on him. She may try to adapt to the world's standards in an attempt to hold on to her husband. But *true* holiness—kindness, fairness, honesty, and genuine devotion to loved ones—can only bless the lives of others and attract them to the ways of God.

Question 7. What does Peter mean when he calls women "the weaker sex"? Author and speaker Jill Briscoe feels that women are made more vulnerable by pregnancy and hormonal changes. J. B. Phillips says women are "physically weaker yet equally heirs of the grace of life." We feel that, in the context, because wives are asked to be submissive (1 Peter 3:1), men must not take advantage of that submission for their own selfish purposes. It could be that all the above are true, and that God is warning men to behave with understanding and sensitivity to their wives.

Questions 9-10. This passage gives advice to believers in an unbelieving world. Perhaps part of that unbelieving world is in your own home, or very close to you.

▪ Study 7/Understanding God's View of Divorce

At the beginning of this study, stress the need for special sensitivity toward those in the group who have been divorced. Remind group members that there are scriptural reasons for divorce and that there are innocent victims. One of the ways you can demonstrate sensitivity is by reserving a time at the end for those who are divorced to share their feelings and to tell how others could be more helpful to them. The purpose of this study is not to judge those who have been divorced, but to help those who are married understand the seriousness of their vows.

Question 4. In contrast, God's way for us is: "Be ye kind one to another, tenderhearted, forgiving one another, even as God for Christ's sake hath forgiven you" (Ephesians 4:32, KJV).

We must keep in mind that in the time of Moses, women were considered property and therefore had no legal rights. Moses' stipulation that a man give his wife a certificate of divorce was actually a means of giving the woman some protection. "The primary thrust of this piece of legislation was to prevent him from taking her again after she had married another man; this would have been an 'abomination before the Lord' (Deuteronomy 24:4). The Law was supposed to deter divorce rather than encourage it. It required a "writing of divorcement"—a public document granting the woman the right to remarry without civil or religious sanction. Divorce could not be done privately" *(The Bible Almanac,* p. 437. Carmel, N.Y.: Guideposts, by special arrangement with Thomas Nelson Publishers, 1980).

Question 5. Scholars disagree on the meaning of Matthew 19:9. The usual "evangelical" stand is that adultery is the only scriptural ground for divorce. Certainly Jesus doesn't demand divorce here. He has already told us in Matthew 18:35 that we should forgive our brother every one of his trespasses. However, if a spouse is unwilling to repent of adultery and thus change his ways, the marriage is already broken in spirit. Then it does seem that the loving counsel would be to permit the wronged party a legal break in the relationship as well—that is, divorce.

Question 7. Old Testament prophecy is filled with metaphors— word pictures of human behavior and God's posture toward us. God used a picture with which people were familiar—that of unfaithfulness in marriage—to teach us about the nature of *spiritual* faithfulness. When we worship and love anything more than God, it is the same as a man leaving his wife of many years and taking another woman as mistress. Although the image of marriage in this case is means of revealing spiritual truth, we are able to see through God's words just how important are the bonds between husband and wife, and how devastating it is when those bonds are broken.

Question 10. The world only gives the person in an unhappy marriage two alternatives: either a life of misery or divorce. With that perspective, many people choose divorce. However, the Lord offers a better way. Two people can come to him, study and apply his Word, and learn to develop a fulfilling and blessed marriage. Even if only one marriage partner comes, that may begin to turn the tide. The Lord sets high standards, but he is also willing to give wisdom and help to meet them.

First Corinthians 7:14 states that the spouse and children of a believer are sanctified or consecrated. This does not mean that they are automatically saved but that they have been set apart for special treatment. Close contact with a believer increases chances for a change in their lives.

Verse 10 tells the believer not to be a deserter. Then verse 11 goes on to say, "but if she [departs] . . ." God's ideal is for a person to stay with the spouse. Is the believer who does depart free to remarry?

Question 11. In a careful and scholarly work, Craig Keener explains that the phrase in 1 Corinthians 7:15, "not be under bondage in such cases" meant that they were free to marry another. He quotes from rabbinical law. The purpose of a writ of divorce was to free them to marry again, if they so chose (Craig Keener, *And Marries Another*. Peabody, Mass.: Hendrickson Publishers, 1991).

■ **Study 8/The Root and Fruit of Love in the Family**

Question 12. A family that merely strives to "be better" without relying on Christ's life flowing through them, will end up in a vicious pattern of adding on "good" activities, growing increasingly busy, and, eventually, living to make a good impression. If we remember that our "goodness" is the result of remaining, living, abiding in the love Christ shows us daily, then we are able to relax our many measurements and love in a way that is only possible by God's grace. One of the first things we must do is stop trying so hard!

■ **Study 9/Spiritual Expression in the Family**

Question 8. Jesus repeats this in the New Testament as being the most important commandment; see Mark 12:28-34.

■ **Study 10/Physical Expression in Marriage**

Question 3. Men and women who are modest don't flaunt themselves or their sexuality in public. This goes against the cultural idea that a man enjoys (with much pride) having on his arm a woman that all other men will lust after. Modesty also calls for some restraint in the kinds of affection a couple expresses to one another in public.

Although most people understand that we shouldn't have sexual relationships outside the marriage, many men and women do not respect the *privacy* of the marriage union; they talk about their spouses to other people. Intimate details about a couple's sex life are shared with friends and family. Men have been notorious for "locker room" talk, but women can act and speak just as inappropriately as they get together over coffee.

Sometimes a person needs an understanding and experienced "listening ear" when sexual problems arise in the marriage. A close friend who can be trusted to keep confidences, an older man or woman—or a married couple both of you respect and trust—a pastor or counselor can offer quality help without violating the privacy of the marriage relationship.

Question 13. Most sexual problems are actually rooted elsewhere—in mental, emotional, or spiritual difficulties. There may be an unforgiven offense or unresolved criticism that gets in the way of sexual attraction. And there may be a physical cause. Couples who are having trouble with their physical relationship should consult with a medical doctor early on. Changes can occur in our bodies (and in our emotions) due to stress, medication, hormonal changes, and other physical irregularities.

■ Study 11/Communication in the Family

Question 3. If we choose to remain honest, even while arguing, we will be kept from making sweeping generalizations or doctoring the facts in order to make ourselves look better. Honesty also helps us to see the situation from another person's viewpoint, and admit when we are wrong.

Question 4. Some kinds of anger—such as anger at injustice or evil—should never completely disappear from our outlook. And many hurts are serious and deep and do not go away easily—or quickly. When Paul urges the Ephesians to deal with their anger before sleep, he speaks of the daily conflicts between people that, left unaddressed, can become inflamed wounds that eventually cause great bitterness. It is possible to disagree with a person without remaining angry. When people act in truthfulness and love, they are able to resolve the hurt between them or make specific plans to deal with the matter at another time when they have had a chance to cool tempers and think more clearly. If we are assured that the other person is at least willing to work with us in resolving the problem, we have no reason to hold on to our anger toward him or her.

▪ Study 12/The Christian Family and Money

Question 10. In 2 Corinthians 8:5, Paul tells how the Macedonians first gave themselves to God. Giving of material things must be voluntary and can only follow the giving of the self to God. This is why it is pointless to try to convince or manipulate a spouse into giving before he or she is ready.

Question 12. While we are freed from the Old Testament tithing law (Romans 10:4), many believers still find 10 percent a helpful guideline. Ron Sider, in *Rich Christians in an Age of Hunger,* gives guidelines for graduated tithes for middle- and upper-income families.

▪ Study 13/Disciplining Our Children

Question 6. A spanking should be approached calmly, in love, and in obedience to God. Larry Christenson writes, "When I saw it was not my anger but God's Word which determined a spanking, I came to it in an entirely different spirit. Not in anger against the child, but in obedience to God. The whole atmosphere was different—and the children sensed it at once. The spankings were surer, harder—and fewer" (Larry Christensen, *The Christian Family.* Minneapolis: Bethany Fellowship, 1970. Used by permission).

Question 9. It is important to note that the Scripture makes a distinction between the "sin that so easily entangles" in Hebrews 12:1, and weaknesses that need to be healed and corrected, as in verses 12-13. Anyone who has been a parent knows that all deficiencies in a child are not the direct result of disobedience or rebellion. For instance, a child who finds it hard to be attentive may simply have other things on his mind—he is distracted by some small thing that would escape the notice of an adult. Children must be trained to do their homework or household chores; they are naturally inclined to put off those things, since they have little sense of time, proportion, or priorities. These are the kinds of areas in which children must be trained; otherwise they grow up unable to act according to principle or manage their time wisely.

Question 10. It is up to the parent to understand the stages of a child's development and what kind of training a child needs in order to build strong principles and healthy habits in life. At different points in their growth, children view the world quite differently than adults do; they have different fears and different needs and follow a different logic. A small child's behavior is seldom a black-and-white issue of obedience or rebellion. A parent who expects the child to act and think like an adult will be ineffective in training that child. Many children are "disabled" due to unreasonable expectations.

Question 13. Ephesians 6:4 says: "And parents, never drive your children to resentment but in bringing them up correct them and guide them as the Lord does" (JB). God "knows how we are formed, he remembers that we are dust" (Psalm 103:14). He suffers through our mistakes because he knows that his thoughts are higher than our thoughts (Isaiah 55:8). Since we receive such merciful and patient treatment from our heavenly Father, we should reflect that kindness to our own children, especially when they are having a difficult time learning a new task or discipline.

WHAT SHOULD WE STUDY NEXT?

To help your group answer that question, we've listed the Fisherman Guides by category so you can choose your next study.

TOPICAL STUDIES

Becoming Women of Purpose, Barton

Building Your House on the Lord, Brestin

Discipleship, Reapsome

Doing Justice, Showing Mercy, Wright

Encouraging Others, Johnson

Examining the Claims of Jesus, Brestin

Friendship, Brestin

The Fruit of the Spirit, Briscoe

Great Doctrines of the Bible, Board

Great Passages of the Bible, Plueddemann

Great People of the Bible, Plueddemann

Great Prayers of the Bible, Plueddemann

Growing Through Life's Challenges, Reapsome

Guidance & God's Will, Stark

Higher Ground, Brestin

How Should a Christian Live? (1,2, & 3 John), Brestin

Marriage, Stevens

Moneywise, Larsen

One Body, One Spirit, Larsen

The Parables of Jesus, Hunt

Prayer, Jones

The Prophets, Wright

Proverbs & Parables, Brestin

Relationships, Hunt

Satisfying Work, Stevens & Schoberg

Senior Saints, Reapsome

Sermon on the Mount, Hunt

The Ten Commandments, Briscoe

When Servants Suffer, Rhodes

Who Is Jesus? Van Reken

Worship, Sibley

BIBLE BOOK STUDIES

Genesis, Fromer & Keyes

Job, Klug

Psalms, Klug

Proverbs: Wisdom That Works, Wright

Ecclesiastes, Brestin

Jonah, Habakkuk, & Malachi, Fromer & Keyes

Matthew, Sibley

Mark, Christensen

Luke, Keyes

John: Living Word, Kuniholm

Acts 1-12, Christensen

Paul (Acts 13-28), Christensen

Romans: The Christian Story, Reapsome

1 Corinthians, Hummel

Strengthened to Serve (2 Corinthians), Plueddemann

Galatians, Titus & Philemon, Kuniholm

Ephesians, Baylis

Philippians, Klug

Colossians, Shaw

Letters to the Thessalonians, Fromer & Keyes

Letters to Timothy, Fromer & Keyes

Hebrews, Hunt

James, Christensen

1 & 2 Peter, Jude, Brestin

How Should a Christian Live? (1, 2 & 3 John), Brestin

Revelation, Hunt

BIBLE CHARACTER STUDIES

Ruth & Daniel, Stokes

David: Man after God's Own Heart, Castleman

Job, Klug

King David: Trusting God for a Lifetime, Castleman

Elijah, Castleman

Men Like Us, Heidebrecht & Scheuermann

Peter, Castleman

Paul (Acts 13-28), Christensen

Great People of the Bible, Plueddemann

Women Like Us, Barton

Women Who Achieved for God, Christensen

Women Who Believed God, Christensen